Four M

The True

Haunting

Copyright © 2014 by Rebecca Patrick-Howard

www.rebeccaphoward.net

Published by Mistletoe Press

All rights reserved. No part of this book may be reproduced, scanned, or distributed in any printed or electronic form without permission.

First Edition: June 2014

Second Edition: August 2014

Printed in the United States of America

Table of Contents

Moving	1
The First Month	10
Sick	19
Betty	25
Uncle Junior	34
Bathroom Breaks	39
The Visitor	45
Nightly Sounds	52
Moving Again	55
The House Today	59
About the author:	69
Windwood Farm excerpt	70

Moving

Growing up, my family had what you'd probably call a fairly typical southern Appalachian view on ghosts: We assumed they existed but unless they were family we tried to steer clear of them. I don't ever remember anyone around me believing in anything like demons or ghouls or some of the scary things in the movies, but it was perfectly fine and acceptable to believe that, should a light in the kitchen flash off and on, Great Aunt Ellen must be up to something. Ghosts were treated almost like an afterthought, a joke. Or maybe just an extended part of the family.

Unless you didn't know the people doing the haunting. Then, things got a little cloudy.

Looking back, I have dozens of memories revolving around supernatural or paranormal explanations of things that went on in our lives. If it was snowing it was because the old woman in Heaven was shaking her featherbed. If there was thunder it was because the angels were bowling. If you couldn't find your hairbrush even though you knew you'd left it in the bathroom, it was because a deceased relative was trying to send you a message. The paranormal was such a part of our world, and our culture, that the *para* part of the word didn't necessarily have to be there.

I was never *scared* of ghosts. Growing up in a time when Scooby Doo taught us that most ghosts were just mean guys in masks, I didn't fear things I couldn't explain because I assume everything could be explained. And besides, even if it was a real ghost I was always told they couldn't hurt you. You just had to be polite, try to figure out what they wanted, and carry on about your business.

At the age of seven, when my grandmother died, we had her wake at our church for two nights before the funeral. Some of the family, who had traveled from faraway states, even slept in the pews. Most everyone spent this time talking, visiting, and even keeping up a prayer vigil.

Me? I gathered some friends and set up a small circle of chairs in one of the Sunday school rooms and tried to hold a little séance to talk to Nana.

It didn't work. I was highly disappointed. My mother was *not* amused.

I also tried hypnotizing my friends a few times because I heard that souls could travel outside the body even when you were still alive and I figured that would be a lot of fun. I must have heard about astral projection somewhere and been confused about how it worked. My friends humored me and told me they were "totally under" and flew through the air and stuff.

As you can see, I was a little bit of a strange child.

I still got scared, of course, but not of ghosts. In a way, the idea of them wasn't that much different than having an imaginary friend and I had a whole slew of those. I would have been happy to glean a sign from Nana, either one of my grandpas, or my Uncle Jimmy. In fact, I did my best to coax them out. I knew they wouldn't hurt me or scare me.

Instead of ghosts, my fears were of intangible things I could never quite put my finger on or explain: the things that *might* lurk in the dark, someone breaking in on us while we were sleeping, the knot on the oak tree that looked somewhat human and always seemed to be watching me...

And then, when I was ten, we moved into the house in Mount Sterling, Kentucky. We only lived there four months, but that was all the time I needed to learn that not every haunting is a good one and that most things to be feared are those that can't be explained.

M0unt Sterling is a small town in central Kentucky. It's not so small that it doesn't have a Wal-Mart (it does), but it's not so big that it has a mall. Most of the restaurants there these days are chains and, like many of the towns its size across the south, the downtown area is drying up and giving way to urban sprawl.

It's a beautiful town, however, with its older homes and well-maintained buildings on Main Street (even if some of them are empty) and the beautiful rolling farmland that surrounds it. You really can't find a lovelier place in most of Kentucky and its charm is widely appreciated by those who visit it every year for the big gathering in October.

The town's big claim to fame is its annual Court Days, where the entire downtown area is taken over by vendors hawking everything from knockoff purses (hopefully not stolen but you never know) to fried apple pies. You really have to see it to believe it. I think one year there was around 100,000 people who attended. I believe it because I'm almost positive I stood in line behind at least half of them for use of the porta potties.

We moved to Mount Sterling for my mother to take a teaching position in the next county over. There weren't any houses available for rent in that county, so we had to look farther afield; thus, we ended up in Mount Sterling. There actually wasn't a lot of possibilities there, either. Still, Mom was happy with what we got. The house we rented was located downtown which made it easy to walk or ride my bike to many of the small stores that were still in existence at the time.

I was excited at the prospect of living downtown. As a child of the 1980s, things were still relatively safe and parents didn't need to keep a close eye on their kids like they do today. Most of the books I read and shows I watched had kids my own age running around downtown, going to the movies with friends and eating at restaurants and I thought that sounded fabulous. Of course, I didn't know anyone there yet and hadn't made any friends but I figured I would eventually and together we could rule the streets with our bikes and roller skates.

I'd never lived in town before, only out in the country, so this was a real novelty to me and I aimed to make the most of it. Times were different then and it was perfectly safe for a ten year old to have run of the neighborhood without worrying about someone killing them or snatching them. Those things still happened, of course, but they happened to other people in other places. The great devil worshipping scare of the early 1980s was mostly over by then so parents weren't so afraid of sending their blue-eyed, blond haired children out to play, only to have them snatched up by cultists looking for fodder for their rituals. (A genuine scare a few years earlier, although it was completely unfounded.)

We were also excited about this move because it brought us closer to where we were originally from, Wolfe County, and we missed living in the area. We'd been living in Martin County for the past several years and both my mother and I were homesick. All in all, it was a happy move for us. It's important to state that upfront. We were glad to be moving back to our home base, excited at the prospect of living downtown in such a pretty area, and thrilled at the idea of a new adventure. We were two gals ready to take on the world, one moving box at a time.

The house itself was interesting. I didn't see it until we started moving in, but I was excited about it because it was old. Built in the 1800s (that's as close to a date as I can get), it was probably a grand house at one time but was falling into neglect by the time we came around.

We didn't care.

We loved the winding staircase, hardwood floors, old stone cellar with multiple rooms, and stained glass windows. I was sure that since it was so old there must be secret passageways in it or a buried treasure or something wonderful and I spent the first few weeks trying to explore it.

I might have been young, but I had a fondness for history that drove some people around me insane. I loved anything to do with the Civil War and antebellum south. I also had a penchant for old, abandoned houses, English manor homes, and things with tunnels. (I blame my mother for my love of the Gothic. I was named after the Daphne DuMaurier book *Rebecca*.) A little quiet and pensive by nature, my idea of fun was to curl up in the corner somewhere with a book. I read everything I could get my hands on and, at that age, saw adventure and romance in just about everything. The old house offered my imagination a wealth of opportunity and I was excited for this next new venture in life with Mom. It wasn't California or Nashville (my choices) but it was something new and different.

From the outside, the house didn't look like much. It was white with a long, thin stretch of a front porch and "half" a story on top which really meant it just had two rooms up there. At one point, the house had been used as apartments so its layout was a little odd and it had two front doors.

Both upstairs bedrooms had what used to be working fireplaces but had since been bricked over. I took one for myself and we used the other one as a guest room. A large stained glass window was at the top of the stairs in the landing and despite the fact that the house was actually pretty big in size, that's all we had on the second floor. On the first floor there were two large bedrooms (one of them a more recent addition built within the past twenty years), a living room, family room, two bathrooms, a utility room, a sitting room, and a large kitchen. One of the bedrooms was at the front of the house; the new bedroom was at the rear, off the kitchen. My mother took the one at the front.

The kitchen was spacious, big enough for a large table and chairs and still with plenty of room left in which to move around. Being an older home, all the rooms had doors that could be opened and closed. "That will be good this winter," Mom muttered as she showed me around on our first day. "We can trap in some of the heat." We were always worrying about utility bills. The last house we lived in didn't have heat and some nights we ended up sleeping at the school or at a friend's. We didn't want to have to go through that again.

The bathrooms boasted claw foot tubs, antique fixtures that were probably original to the house, and wallpaper that looked at least fifty years old. When you peeled it back other layers were revealed behind it, like flipping through a deck of cards.

Surrounded by some of these old world charms, I immediately began pretending I lived back in some old south time period and this was my plantation house. It didn't matter to me that we had neighbors on either side of us. With the overgrown backyard I could barely see them. I think I even started sleeping in my mother's nightgowns, pretending I was a southern belle getting ready to have her coming out party.

As a child, I didn't see most of the neglect. On the outside, the paint was peeling, the porch was sagging, and there were bald spots in the grass. On the inside, the whole house could probably have done with some re-wiring, the grout in the bathroom needed to be replaced, there were scuff marks in the kitchen floor, and some of the rooms slanted a little to one side.

I still thought it was probably the nicest house I'd ever lived in.

The First Month

Our first couple of weeks were uneventful as we tried to unpack and get settled into our new home. We had a lot of stuff and even though it was a large house we had trouble making everything fit. In fact, one bone of contention we had right off the bat was that our landlord, an old man who was hard of hearing, actually started bringing in his friends to give them a tour of the house just to show them how much stuff we had. He had a habit of doing this at all hours of the day and night and not knocking first. He caught us both in awkward phases of undress and bathing. I can still remember lying in bed, half asleep, and hearing the front door open. "Cover up!" Mom would yelp, afraid that my (her) nightgown had slipped and I might be exposing something.

She nipped the little house tours in the bud pretty quickly.

Other than our landlord's guided tours of our stuff, only two things of note happened within the first couple of weeks: the exploration of the cellar and the man.

The former happened to me. I was disappointed to find that there were not any hidden staircases or treasure chests (I was really into Nancy Drew at the time) but I wasn't going to give up so easily. There had to be something remarkable about the house. It was too cool not to have a secret! I found it downstairs. The house had a cellar, only accessible by going outside and walking around the side of the house, made of stone with dirt floors and even though we couldn't put anything down there, I liked to play in it.

I suppose I should mention that I had no real fear of dark places at this point. I didn't like nighttime and *that* kind of dark, but I was perfectly fine with basements, caves, and darkness during the daylight hours. One of our favorite forms of cheap entertainment was to go for long drives and find abandoned houses we could take pictures of. We'd shimmy through windows, crawl around on all fours on dirty floors, and fight all kinds of vermin and insects just to get interesting pictures and "explore." And I'd climbed around in caves and dark hollows just about all my life. It was only when I was trying to go to sleep at night that my imagination got the best of me.

There were three rooms in the cellar and the first two were dreadfully dark. They were even a little too dark for me. I at least liked to see my hand in front of my face when I was playing. They had tiny windows, but the windows were covered up with vines and dirt so no light could penetrate through them. I usually passed through these rooms quickly and went on to the last room.

The third room was a little bit lighter and depending on the time of day you went in there you could get a pale slant of light shining through the small cracked glass into the middle of the floor. I was never afraid of spiders or snakes (I probably thought we couldn't get any since we were in town) and the only thing that ever really freaked me out was the small pile of rodent bones in the corner of the room. I just pretended they weren't there.

For hours, I would play with My Little Pony or Barbie down there in that dirt-floored room, oblivious to the outside world. It was cool there in the cellar, cooler than it was in the house, and nobody bothered me. I liked being alone and having my own secret place. Mom would never go down there. The small flight of stairs were too steep for her arthritic legs and she didn't like the damp, dark, closed-in nature of the rooms. Besides, she had a lot to do in the house, what with all the unpacking and such. Down in the cellar I had my own little world and could play as long as I wanted to. I made up pretend games, played with my imaginary friend, and sang songs to myself. I was a little lonely, but still felt as though I was living in an adventure so that helped.

One day, however, as I was leaving I noticed something out of the corner in my eye in the first room. It was a staircase! I don't know why I'd never seen it before, but the rickety stairs definitely led up from the cellar into what was probably the kitchen. The opening where they would have come out at was closed off.

I couldn't wait to run back up and tell my mom.

"Hey," I hollered as I ran into the kitchen to find her putting away canned food in the cabinet. "Did you know there used to be stairs here in this room going down to the cellar?"

"Really?" she asked. "Well, I guess that makes sense. I wondered why there wasn't a way to get down there other than from outside."

So I took her down and gave her the tour. The stairs were too fragile to walk on, but I was extremely excited at the discovery, which wasn't nearly as good as a secret tunnel or passageway but was pretty darn close.

Later that evening, she put me to work putting away more food. There was a very small hole in the middle of the wall with a door on it. When you opened the door, two shelves ran back into the walls. They were wide enough to put food on but the whole setup was very unusual. If you put anything too far back you wouldn't be able to reach them. "I don't know why they put this here," Mom complained. She gave me the job of filling it up because it was such a hassle. I usually got the messy or inconvenient tasks.

While I organized packages of spaghetti and sauce, I noticed something I hadn't before about the shelves–they came out! It was a day of discoveries for me. Using a flashlight, I looked behind the shelves and, sure enough, could see the outline of what used to be another opening. When I pointed the flashlight down, I could see the remnants of a rope.

I called my mother again. "Look," I said, pointing. "I think this is one of those dumbbell things that people used to put food on."

"What? Dumbbell? You mean a dumbwaiter?" she asked.

"Yeah, that. And look, there's another door!"

We eventually figured out that it must have been set up so that you could pass food from the kitchen into the dining room without having to leave the room. Of course, by the time we lived there, it had all been boarded up and papered over. (And we were using the dining room for our living room.) From down in the cellar, however, you could still see where the dumbwaiter used to land.

"So rich people must have lived here," I said with certainty, feeling a little smug. "Why else would they be sending food to the basement if they didn't have servants to get it?"

"I guess you've got a point there," Mom said thoughtfully. "Or, maybe they were feeding people down in the basement."

"What for? You mean like they kidnapped them?" I asked in wonder. I was very much into kidnapping stories at the time.

"No, like maybe slaves. The owners said this house was part of the Underground Railroad," she explained.

We spent the rest of the evening discussing the particulars of the Railroad and how it had worked. Now, I was even more excited. I couldn't believe that I was getting to live in a house that might have actually been a part of real history.

We later discovered that there used to be a door between my mother's room and the sitting room. It was also boarded up and papered over. It might not have been quite as good as a secret passageway, but I was happy our house had secrets.

Two weeks after moving in, a knock on our door came in the middle of the afternoon. I opened it to find a nice looking young man in glasses. He smiled pleasantly at me and asked if my parents were home. I got my mother.

"Hi," he started, "I know this is going to sound strange but my grandmother lived here when I was a little kid and this is the first time I've been back in years. I was wondering if you'd let me walk around and look at the house."

Now, to most people this might have sounded strange but we're friendly people and, the fact is, we had done the very same thing a few weeks before. When I was born I was brought home to a house in Mount Sterling. We moved out not too long after that so I didn't remember the house. When we returned to Mount Sterling, however, my mother had taken me there and we'd knocked on the door and asked if we could look around. They let us in and gave us a tour, even though they didn't know us from Adam.

Who were we to refuse this guy?

Mom was in the middle of something but thought nothing of letting me walk around with the young man. He was friendly and talkative and filled me with all kinds of stories about his time there at the house with his grandmother. He pointed out the rooms she lived in (the house was two apartments at that time) and the antics he'd gotten into. He even showed me how he used to slide down the bannister.

I liked the man and nothing about him sent up any red flags my way but I couldn't help but notice that every time we went into a room he appeared to be looking for something. He'd stand there, stop, look around, and walk to the fireplace or the closet or something and act like he was trying to find something but wasn't sure where he'd left it. I pointed this out to my mother before we went down to the cellar and she followed us the rest of the way. "Maybe he's just remembering things," she whispered. "He might just be looking at the room and thinking about the things he used to do in it."

In the cellar, I showed him the "secret" staircase and the dumbwaiter. He remembered them since he'd also played down there as a kid. "I liked playing here in the cellar, too," he smiled. "It's cool and dark. Of course, when I stayed here there was furniture down here and all these vines were gone."

I wanted to put furniture down there, too, but we were afraid it would flood. And things were awfully dirty down there anyway. I always came up filthy.

I was a little sad to see him go. I missed having my friends around and it got kind of lonely playing there by myself. He was the first company we'd had since we moved in.

A few days later, Mom was in the utility room doing laundry. I'm not sure what the room was originally used for but it was one of the most neglected places in the house.

Both of us could look at just about any building and see the good in it, even if it was on its last legs, but this room looked like it might cave in at any moment. You could see the wires coming out of the electrical outlets and nobody had even bothered to paint or paper the walls in years. A few of the floorboards really squeaked and I was afraid to walk too hard on them in fear I might go crashing through to the cellar. We didn't use the utility room much.

At any rate, Mom had a load in the washer and one in the dryer and was busying herself in the kitchen when she just happened to go in and check on them. A good thing, too, because sparks were shooting up the wall where the dryer was plugged in. The inside of the wall was on fire and the room was starting to fill with smoke.

It took a miracle and quick thinking on Mom's part to get the fire out, but she finally managed. Another few minutes and it might have caught some of the old boards and insulation and sent the whole house up in flames.

That incident shook her and doing laundry was never the same after that. It also meant the bloom was off the rose as far as the house went. Suddenly, moving in there didn't feel like such a good idea, even if it was only $300 a month.

Sick

Mom understood how much I missed my friends and once we'd at least made a path with our boxes through the house she invited my friend Teri to come and stay a week with us. Teri lived back in Martin County and we'd spent almost every day together that summer until we moved. I was brown as a butterball from all the time we'd spent at the local swimming pool and suddenly being without her was like losing a limb. I really thought I'd have made friends by then, but the only other girl on my street was a girl named Olivia who lived in a mansion (a real mansion) four doors down. She was nice enough but told me that when school started she would have to come and pick out my clothes for me because she wasn't convinced I'd be able to match them on my own.

Two weeks later and I was still trying to think of a comeback to that insult.

I was so excited at the thought of having my friend come and stay with me that I couldn't sleep for several nights. I stayed up, reading and watching VHS tapes since we didn't have cable. Teri was happy to come and stay with us, too, especially when I told her about all the fun things we could do downtown and how I had an extra bike for her to ride.

On her second night at the house, however, I became very ill. I hadn't missed a day of school in two years, but I unexpectedly woke up in the middle of the night, vomiting violently and with a raging fever. It went on for some days without any relief. Our living room couch let out into a bed and Mom made a place to sleep for Teri and me there so I could be close to the bathroom. I wasn't able to eat, walk, or bathe without help from someone and the days soon began to bleed together as I felt as though I'd never be well again. My fever spiked to 104 degrees at one point but since we didn't have our insurance yet we couldn't afford to take me to the doctor. I was in and out of consciousness for the most part, first feeling wretchedly hot and then frightfully cold. Everything hurt and as I moaned and groaned in pain and clutched at my stomach I found myself praying aloud for some kind of relief. In the middle of the sickness I felt horribly guilty for not being much fun for Teri but she was understanding, even as a child, and tried to help Mom take care of me.

The move had taken most of our money and if we wanted a treat, like French fries somewhere, we had to roll pennies we found around the house. I probably should have gone to the doctor, but we all thought it would pass and I'd improve at any minute. The sickness was relentless, though. I called out for Mom, for Nana, and pleaded for help. There wasn't much anyone could do.

It was extremely difficult for me to eat or drink anything but Mom was hell-bent on getting Gatorade into me, always sure that it was the miracle cure for anything that ailed you. On the third day, we ran out of it and she left Teri with me while she ran out to the store to pick some up. She used change she found around the house to pick some up.

I was still fading in and out of consciousness at that point and couldn't tell you if it was day or night. We kept the curtains drawn in the living room so the room remained dark. It helped me sleep.

I remember sitting up and feeling alone. "Teri," I called. She appeared from the kitchen, her eyes kind of wide and upset. I believe she was half afraid of me by then.

"Yeah?"

"I feel like I could eat something. Do you think you could make me a baked potato?" It was the one thing that had more or less stayed down and my stomach was in pain from being empty. She'd been making them for herself over the past few days, too, just by poking holes in them with a fork and then popping them in the microwave for a few minutes.

"Sure," she replied. "Do you want anything on it other than butter and pepper?"

"No, that's all. Thank you."

When she left the room I laid back down and must have drifted off to sleep again. I felt warm and woozy, like I was floating through the room. What seemed like hours later I heard her scream. There's nothing like the sound of a ten year old girl screaming to bring you back from the brink of death.

Teri, in her ponytail and nine year old scrawny knees poking out from her cutoffs, was standing there at the side of the bed, looking down at me in horror. A plate was balanced in her hand. "What's the matter?" I asked as I tried to sit up and failed. I just didn't have the strength to move.

"I saw–I thought I saw–I–" she could barely get the words out and her face was ashen. I took the plate from her and set it on the bed next to me.

"What did you see?" Now I was starting to feel afraid and it dawned on me that we were in the house alone. Could I get out if someone came in on us?

"Your grandmother!" she finally blurted out. "She was sitting right there on the bed with you, touching you! Looking at you!"

I don't think I need to mention that my grandmother had passed away three years before.

"Are you sure?" I asked, looking at the barren spot in the bed she was pointing to.

"Yes! Just like the pictures you have of her. It was the same person," she insisted.

Well, that made me feel a little better. In relief, I closed my eyes and smiled. If Nana was in the house looking out for me then I'd feel better in no time at all! After comforting Teri and assuring her that if she had seen Nana everything was okay because she was like my guardian angel, I put in a new movie for her, ate my potato, and fell back asleep. Hours later, I woke up feeling rested and fine. My nausea, aches and pains, and fever were all gone.

I wouldn't be the only one to get sick from the mysterious virus. Mom and Teri were to come down with it as well. Luckily, we got Teri home before hers became too bad. It was very difficult for a ten year old to take care of her mother, though. Mom was down for almost a week with it and during that time I had to do most of the cleaning, cooking, and whatever else needed to be done. I blamed the house. I knew it was silly to blame a house for being sick but I hadn't been really sick in years, and neither had Mom, and now here we were fighting something bad off. I couldn't go out and play for very long because Mom might need something. I didn't have any friends around, we couldn't afford to have cable or a telephone, and I felt trapped. I couldn't wait for school to start.

I never saw any mysterious visitors sitting next to Mom on the bed, nor did she, but she did have some pretty wicked dreams. Unfortunately, right before she got sick we'd watched the movie "Tremors"–the Sci-Fi movie with the big worm things in the ground? Well, apparently in her feverish state she woke up at one point and swore they were in the walls. She could see the walls moving and waving under their weight and called out for help, certain they would break free and come gobble her up.

Betty

One of the perks of living in Mount Sterling was that we got to visit my cousin Betty regularly. Betty was an interesting soul, not just because she was family and I tend to think we're all kind of unique, but because of the situation she was in. She had an adult son named Brian and when he was nine years old he'd fallen into a comatose state for no known reason. He couldn't move or speak intelligibly (Betty said she could understand him) yet his eyes were open and he often seemed aware of what was going on. He'd been like that for almost twenty years.

Rather than send him to live in a facility, like most everyone encouraged her to do, Betty had a hospital bed brought into her home and took care of him around the clock. He was hooked up to a central line and she changed all of his IVs, diapers, and took care to ensure he didn't get bed sores or atrophy. She even slept in the room with him. Betty refused to leave the house for anything other than his doctor visits. He often came down with infections and illnesses, despite her exquisite care of him. (He had to be taken by ambulance when he left the house.) If Betty needed something from the store, somebody brought it to her. She ordered her towels, decorations, and other products from magazines like Home Interior. It had been more than a decade since she's shopped in a store herself, gone to the movies, or eaten in a restaurant. As a result, she was a recluse in that she never left, but she was so likable that she always had tons of visitors and her house was never empty. With her loud laugh, wicked sense of humor, and ability to make anyone feel welcome in her home she was never without company.

And Betty was a mean cook. She could make anything country-style you wanted.

I noticed that the longer we lived in our new house, the more frequent our trips to Betty's became. I also noticed that our stays became longer. I wasn't blind. I just wasn't sure why this was happening.

In the beginning, we'd go for a chat and stay an hour. Soon, we were going two or three times a week and staying until the late hours of the evening, even eating supper with her. We were a little tight on money, so I figured it might have been for the benefit of the food. Betty always insisted we stay for whatever meal was coming up next and our cupboards were often bare.

I didn't mind going to Betty's at all. Her grandkids were my age (they were also cousins) and they stayed with her a lot. I enjoyed having someone to play with. I am a little ashamed to admit that Brian scared me some, however. I didn't remember a time when he was able to talk, walk, and eat like a healthy man so to me he'd always been the person in the hospital bed that moaned and shouted a lot–never any words I could understand. Betty referred to him as "Baby Brian" and had her grandkids convinced that God protected him as something special. Indeed, a tornado had ripped through Mount Sterling a few years earlier and the kids hid under Brian's hospital bed. Several houses on her road were destroyed. The pictures in every room in her house were shaken off the walls. Not a thing was touched in Brian's room.

But back to our visits...

One afternoon we were getting ready to visit Betty and I remembered I'd left something upstairs in my bedroom. I didn't use my bedroom for sleeping at the time. We were sleeping in the guest room next to it because my room was still full of boxes and Mom hadn't unpacked hers yet, either. I ran up to get it while Mom waited downstairs in the car for me. I wasn't that excited about getting my room cleaned up and ready for sleeping. The idea of staying in it made me nervous. The first few days it had seemed fine. I played in there, tried to organize things, and decorated. Sure, it was hot and stuffy but nothing I couldn't handle.

Then, something turned me off. I constantly felt like someone was watching me. Little movements would catch from the corner of my eye and I'd turn, only to find that nobody was there. It was an uncomfortable feeling, like I was being spied on by a teacher or parent. It made me feel like I was doing something wrong. I often talked to myself when I was playing with my Barbies or toys but when I was upstairs I kept my voice low, hushed, as if someone was listening to the words I was saying and weighing them.

In the beginning, I laughed it off and joked about it and even hesitantly called out to Nana, but received no reply. Instead, the hairs on my arms stood up and the utter stillness that met me in return made me think someone, or something, was hiding rather than not present at all.

There was also something a little stifling about the room, a little thick. I thought it might have just been because we didn't have central heat and air and the air conditioner didn't always reach all the way up there. But it felt different than mere heat. Sometimes I had difficulty catching my breath, as though I was chest-deep in water and had to hoist myself out to get the air deep into my lungs. When I spent time at the swimming pool the heat outside wrapped around me like a flower, warming me from head to toe and making me feel alive. This heat wrapped around me like a thick, scratchy blanket. I was starting to have misgivings about choosing that room for mine.

At any rate, there was a little rocking chair with a red velvet seat cover in the corner of the room. My dad had reupholstered it for me the year before last for Christmas. The red in the chair caught my eye as I was leaving the room and, as I turned back around, I was startled to see it gently rocking back and forth.

I was so surprised to see it moving that I couldn't take my eyes off it and stopped in my tracks. There was nothing in the room touching it and no air currents or wind strong enough to reach it to make it rock. It was just...rocking. It wasn't a gentle movement, but a particular rocky motion, as though someone was making it move on purpose. It stopped and started in spurts, disjointed, and I was mesmerized by it. I stood rooted to the floor for at least thirty seconds, although it felt much longer, and then it came to an abrupt stop. I ran down the stairs and out the door.

Several nights later, my cousin April (Betty's granddaughter) was spending the night with me. We were upstairs in my room, playing, when April suddenly shrieked, causing me to drop the doll whose hair I was brushing. The radio was on in the corner and George Strait was softly singing about drinking champagne and all I could think of was that I was annoyed with April for interrupting the song.

"What? What's the matter?" I asked, irritated. I thought she'd been bit by a spider or something. I'd seen a lot of those around lately. Big, brown things the size of my hand.

"Look!" she pointed, gesturing wildly with her hand.

The red rocking chair was moving again, this time even faster. April jumped over a pile of dolls and stood by me, clasping my arm in fright. She buried her face in my shoulder and whimpered a little, but all I could do was watch in fascination. As we stood there and listened to George sing and watched the chair moving on its own accord, neither one of us could move. "What's going on? What's doing that?" she whispered.

"I don't know," I whispered back. The chair was pointed at us so not only was it rocking, it had turned almost completely around. Whatever was there was watching us and wanted us to know it. I was sure of that. This frightened me more than the actual movement. I knew someone was in the room with us just as sure as I would have been had I actually seen a person in the chair. And it wasn't a good feeling. This was not Great Aunt Ellen, Nana, or one of my grandpas. This was something else. And I was scared.

Then, just as soon as it seemed to start, it stopped. The chair came to a gentle standstill and ceased motion, like someone had laid a tender hand on it and steadied it.

With that, we both took off and ran downstairs. I didn't even stop and turn the radio off. It played for three days until my mom finally went in the room and turned it off.

A week later we were over at Betty's when Mom excused herself from the table and went to the bathroom. Betty and I were sitting at the kitchen table, eating ice cream and talking. She was Mom's age, but I felt like I could talk to her like a friend.

Sensing a good time to bring it up, I took a chance. "Betty," I started. "Do you think a house can be haunted by someone who isn't your relative?"

"I think so," she said, very serious-like. "I think a house can be haunted by just about anyone. Do you think yours is?"

I quickly told her about the rocking chair and about some of the other things I'd seen and heard. They hadn't been big, just things out of the corner of my eye, but they'd been enough to spook me. I was starting to have nightmares. I was also starting to look over my shoulder a lot and no longer enjoyed playing in the cellar alone.

"What makes you think it's not your nana or someone you know doing it?" she asked. I loved how she wasn't making fun of me and acted like I was an adult.

"Because Nana wouldn't scare me," I answered. "She would show herself or say something. She wouldn't make me scared."

"I don't think most ghosts try to scare people. I think maybe they just can't help it. We're the ones that get afraid of them because we don't understand their world and what they want."

"I don't know," I shook my head. "I think there's something in our house and it doesn't want us there. And it's trying to scare us on purpose. Or trying to scare me. It doesn't feel right."

Betty took this answer in stride and agreed. "I see what you're saying," she said. "But maybe these ghosts don't want to hurt you. Maybe they just don't know what else to do. Have you tried talking to them?"

No, I hadn't, but I thought I might try that next.

A few days later I was in the living room, alone, while Mom was outside bringing things in from the car. A noise in the kitchen got my attention and thinking it might have been our cat (she wouldn't come inside but maybe she'd changed her mind) I went in to check. Two of the cabinet doors I'd previously closed were standing wide open.

Seeing my opportunity to try out Betty's advice, I planted myself firmly on the floor and took a deep breath. "Hello!" I called. "How are you? I'm Rebecca."

In unison, both cabinet doors slammed shut and a sound I can only describe as a low growl filled the air. I tripped over my own feet as I scurried out of the room and raced to the front door, nearly colliding with Mom.

I didn't try to speak to the ghosts again.

Uncle Junior

Six weeks after moving into the house, we received word that my uncle Junior and his girlfriend would be coming to stay with us.

I should take a moment here to describe my Uncle Junior. At the time, he was a tattooed truck driver who liked his beer, country music, and his Native American girlfriend (Johnnie) equally. This was not a weak man; this was a man who'd ran away from home as a young teenager and joined a tribe on an Indian Reservation. He had skin like leather, talked with grit in his voice, and had spent time in jail with Chuck Berry for trying to sneak underage girls across the state line.

Anyway, Uncle Junior and Johnnie (not technically my aunt since Junior was still married to my Aunt Anneda) came to stay with us. They were planning on being there for a month, at least.

We prepared for their arrival a week in advance. At this time, we were sleeping upstairs in the guest room. Mom still hadn't completely unpacked her bedroom downstairs yet but the guest room didn't have much in it.

Plus, I could play in my bedroom while she was in bed. I'd stopped that, of course, with the whole rocking chair incident. Now I mostly played with my toys in the family room which was still full of boxes but kind of felt like a cave.

In preparation for the arrival of Uncle Junior and Johnnie we tried to clean the house the best we could, went grocery shopping, and planned some things we could do with them while they were there. We figured on putting them in Mom's room downstairs when they arrived so they could be close to the bathroom while we continued to sleep upstairs.

Something changed that plan, though.

One morning, I awoke to an awful sight on our bed sheets. It was still summertime and hot so we weren't sleeping with more than a flat sheet over us. This one was white and although it had been clean when we went to bed, now it was sprinkled with flecks of red. It looked as though someone had taken a pepper shaker and dusted us with red paint. I touched the spots but they were dry.

"Mom?" I shook her awake. "Mom, what is this?"

My mother sat up and looked at the sheets and gasped. "Are you okay?" she asked me as she took hold of me and searched my face and hands.

"Yeah, why?"

"Because that's blood," she pointed. And, on closer inspection, she proved to be right. Some of the spots were bright red, others were almost black, but they definitely looked like blood stains. They weren't any larger than a pin prick in most places but a few dollops were the size of a quarter.

Neither one of us had any injuries that would have bled during the night, nor did we have any signs that our noses or mouths might have caused such a thing to happen. The sheet was covered, though.

"Well, maybe it's just a fluke. Maybe it was there from the cat or something and we didn't notice it when we went to bed," Mom suggested. But she didn't sound completely convinced. We quickly tossed the sheet off us and threw it in the floor. Neither one of us wanted to touch it to take it downstairs.

The next night, we changed the sheets on our bed and went to sleep.

When I awoke that next morning, I was greeted by the same sight: Our top sheet was once again covered with flecks of blood.

"Um, Mom," I woke her up again. "The blood is back."

For three nights in a row we woke up covered in blood spots. Finally, we gave it up and decided to sleep downstairs in her room. It was almost organized in time for Uncle Junior's arrival anyway so we might as well take it.

They could have the guest room. It might not have been very hospitable of us, but we couldn't sleep in there anymore.

Uncle Junior and Johnnie loved the house. They loved the old rooms, the floors, the staircase, and even the cellar. They looked forward to spending a month with us. During that first week we tried to make it fun for them as we ate out at restaurants, went shopping, and even went hiking at a local waterfall. At night, Uncle Junior would sometimes get out his guitar and we'd sit there in the kitchen while he sang songs like "Does Fort Worth Ever Cross Your Mind" and "Don't Close Your Eyes."

Neither Junior nor Johnnie ever said anything bad about the house. They both continued to profess their love for it. Two weeks into their stay, however, they packed up and informed us they had to leave. When we woke up to go to school that morning, Uncle Junior was already packing his bags while Johnnie sat at the kitchen table, nervously chewing on her fingernail. She wouldn't look at us in the eye. We were sad and disappointed. I wanted to cry. I had so been looking forward to their stay and couldn't understand why they would simply leave without talking about it with us first.

"Is everything okay?" Mom asked Uncle Junior as he loaded up his car. He was on his way back to Oklahoma. "Did something happen?"

"Brenda," he said, "it's not you. You didn't do anything. We just can't stay in that house anymore."

They wouldn't tell us what happened or what finally made them decide to cut their visit short, but by the end of the day they were gone. Unfortunately, Uncle Junior passed away without ever sharing his story with us.

Bathroom Breaks

I was ten years old when we moved into the house.

Except for a few times when I was sick and couldn't stop the nausea or control my stomach, I'd never been one to have bathroom issues in the middle of the night. I'd never wet the bed, for instance. I was as easy to potty train as any other child probably is.

But something happened in that house that would cause me a major setback.

The first night I wet the bed we laughed about it. "Did you dream you were peeing and couldn't stop?" Mom laughed. She changed the sheets and blankets while I cleaned up in the bathroom. "Don't worry about it. It happens to me sometimes. We'll just clean it up." I was embarrassed, but there wasn't anything I could do about it. I didn't even know I was peeing until I woke up on cold sheets.

School had started by then. I was in the fifth grade. What would my new friends say if they knew I'd wet the bed? I was in the double digits now at the age of ten. I wasn't a baby anymore.

A few nights later, however, it happened again.

"Well, maybe you need to stop drinking anything before you go to bed," Mom suggested.

So I stopped all liquids at around 8:00 pm. Since we didn't usually go to bed until about midnight, that was a long time to stay up without a drink but I thought anything was worth a shot. I hated waking up with that cold, wet feeling and having to get up and groggily change the sheets when my eyes weren't even all the way open.

I peed in the bed again. This time, Mom didn't think it was funny. At 3:00 am while she was changing the sheets, she grumbled and fussed. I sat on the toilet in the bathroom and cried, frustrated because I didn't understand why I kept doing it.

"Are you going to the bathroom before you go to bed?" she asked me. "You need to go before you go to sleep!"

"Yes!" I shouted back. "I go right before I go to bed and I'm not drinking anything, either." That time I'd felt the pee almost as soon as it started coming but I hadn't been able to stop it. Even though I knew what I was doing, my body continued to stay asleep and I just couldn't wake it up in time to go to the bathroom.

It continued to happen for the next couple of weeks. Sometimes, Mom wouldn't even change the sheets. We got to where we were so tired of getting up and changing the bedding that she'd just put a towel down to cover up the wet spot and I'd go back to sleep. After all, we were running out of blankets and sheets and doing laundry didn't hold the thrill it used to, now that we were afraid of burning the house down.

One night, I peed in the bed and she changed the sheets and then I went back to bed and it happened again that very same night.

Neither one of us were happy campers.

Eventually, the nightly bed-wetting stopped the same way it started. I'd gone to the doctor and he couldn't find any reason why I might be suddenly having the problems. When Mom was out of the room, though, he came back in and asked me the usual questions: Was anyone bothering me? Was anyone touching me in a way they shouldn't be? Was I afraid? "Afraid of what?" I asked.

"Of anything, really. Of going to the bathroom," he said. "It might be that you're afraid to get up and go to the bathroom so your mind won't let your body wake up."

I thought about that for a long time. It made sense. Was I really afraid?

Yes, I was. The house was scaring me. I was afraid to talk to Mom about it, but I felt uneasy there. I couldn't always put my finger on why I felt afraid, but now even just stepping inside the front door felt like someone was throwing a blanket over my head and trying to suffocate me.

A few weeks after Uncle Junior left, our friend Jackie came to stay with us. We'd met him and his wife years ago when they were both in college and he was like family to us. Several years younger than Mom, he was like the brother I never had and I always enjoyed his visits. Since he and his wife were relocating back to Kentucky from Florida he asked if he could stay with us for awhile until he found work and a place to live. His wife would be living with her family in West Virginia.

    I was ecstatic at the thought of having Jackie around. He was more fun than a barrel of monkeys; I mean it. Always up to some kind of hijinks, there was never a dull moment when he was around. He could make an adventure out of anything and even a simple bike ride around the neighborhood would turn into something epic. And he'd have me in stitches laughing. Jackie and I had develop dour own secret language and often talked to one another in code. He played video games with me, rented movies for us to watch, and cooked dinner most nights.

Jackie's positive energy had the house brightening up in no time. We were so happy to have him there. This was probably around the time the bedwetting stopped.

One night, however, I woke up with horrible stomach pains. The cramps were unlike anything I'd ever had before and as I rolled around in the bed, clutching my stomach, I was sure something was rupturing and I was dying. It felt like I was going to have a bowel movement so I finally decided going to the bathroom might help. I wanted to wake Mom up and tell her, but after the bedwetting episodes I was afraid. I didn't want her to get mad at me. So, holding onto my stomach, I crept down the dark hall into the dark room and flipped on the light.

As I sat on the toilet in the quiet house, though, and tried to make something happen I felt helpless and powerless. The lights were off in the rest of the house so I stared into a sea of darkness, unable to see anything past the bathroom door. The bathroom with its cheery light felt small, unguarded. There were noises in the house; noises I'd never paid a lot of attention to at night. I could hear creaks and whispers, what sounded like footsteps walking above me in what was our guest room. (Jackie was sleeping in the back of the house off the kitchen.) As the noises closed in around me, I could do nothing but sit there on the toilet with my eyes closed, waiting for my body to finish what it needed to do. I felt helpless in my position, unable to get up and move. As my stomach wracked in cramps and my bowels ruptured into the toilet I had no defenses and could only listen and wonder about what would happen next. Something terrible felt just inches away, right outside the door, but I couldn't do anything about it. At any moment I imagined something long, shadowy, and terrible would slither inside and reach for me, grasping my foot or my arm and pulling me into some dark, dreadful abyss I'd never be able to escape from. I'd never been so scared in my life but I didn't dream of crying out to my mother. I knew she'd be angry for waking her up.

I ended up having to get up three more times that night to go to the bathroom and each experience was worse than the one before it. I cried as I ran from our bed of safety, through the dark hall, to the illuminated bathroom. The dark grabbed at me and pulled at my nightgown, whispered at my feet, and whipped at my face with its icy tentacles. At one point, there even seemed to be footsteps pacing back and forth outside the bathroom door as someone waited for me to step outside. My body felt used, drained. I slumped on the toilet, my head leaning on the wall, as I tried to find the courage to go back to the bedroom one last time. I begged for Jackie or Mom to wake up on their own and come and rescue me but everyone remained asleep.

The Visitor

With Jackie in the house, life continued on at some sort of normal pace. My mother taught at the school I attended so we'd ride in together every morning. It was often late in the afternoon before we got back to the house and Jackie, who found a job nearby selling jewelry, would return a little after us. Together, the four of us would eat dinner and talk about our day and maybe watch a movie or go for a walk.

 Those were lean times in terms of money for all of us. It took Jackie several weeks to get his first paycheck and everyone knows a teacher doesn't go into that line of work for the pay. For almost a month we lived off of baked potatoes, piled high with whatever spices we could throw on them and cheese.

 It was starting to get late into the fall and the house wasn't easy to heat. We quit going upstairs almost altogether and lived primarily in the living room, kitchen, and two downstairs bedrooms. Luckily, with it being an old house we were able to shut the doors to the rooms we weren't using. A space heater kept us warm and took the edge off while we piled our beds high with comforters and feather mattresses.

It might have been a depressing time, eating mostly potatoes and huddling together in cold rooms, but it wasn't. In fact, it was fun. For at least a little while the shadows of the house were held back while we sat together as a family in the old kitchen at the primitive table, seeing who could pile the most cheese on top of their baked potatoes and who could come up with the most outlandish recipes with what little ingredients we had left in the cupboards.

Walks around the neighborhood with the falling leaves and old, brick houses became after-dinner adventures for Jackie and me and we both fantasized about the day we might be able to afford something grand ourselves. People were starting to decorate for Halloween and pumpkins, scarecrows, and witches began showing up on front porches and sidewalks.

I mostly went to bed at night feeling snug and content, despite the fact that a cloud of unease seemed to hover above us. Mom must have felt it, too, because the house was still littered with boxes. We'd never unpacked the sitting room or family room and her bedroom looked as though a tornado had gone through it. We seemed to be in a constant state of readiness; readiness for what, I wasn't sure.

On one bitterly cold evening Mom and I sat in the living room with all the doors closed. I had a blanket covering my lap and I sat by the window, reading a book. Mom was on the other side of the room, also engrossed in her own papers. We didn't have the television on but the portable kerosene heater was going at almost full blast.

Suddenly, the sound of the front door opening interrupted my thoughts. I shrugged it off, assuming it was Jackie. He was, after all, due home at any moment.

I continued reading but kept an ear out for him. Sure enough, I heard his footsteps coming down the short hallway and then pause outside the living room door. I looked up with a smile, ready to greet him, but was surprised when I heard the footsteps turn away from the door and start back towards the staircase. A few moments later, sounds could be heard above us as someone intentionally walked back and forth in what was my room.

The blood in me all but drained as I quietly laid my book down and looked at my mother. "Mom," I said nervously. "Did you hear that?"

I expected her to look up at me, smile, and say she hadn't heard a thing. But she didn't. Instead, she rose to her feet and replied, "It must be Jackie. He's just playing a trick on us."

But there was no reason for him to be upstairs and Jackie would never try to scare me like that. I knew in my heart it wasn't Jackie. Nor did I think it was some long-dead relative coming back to say a nightly "hello." Mom's acknowledgement of the noise scared me almost more than the noise itself; it meant she had heard it as well and was disturbed by it, whereas a second ago I might have thought it was just in my head.

Mom quickly walked to the door and opened it, peering out into the darkness of the hallway. We'd forgotten to leave a light on. "Put your shoes on, Rebecca," she said very loudly.

The walking above us stopped.

"They *are* on," I pointed out, confused.

Turning around, she "shushed" me and continued across the hall to the bathroom where she flipped that light on as well. There was a slight creak overhead, as though someone or something might be waiting for our next move.

"Let's go!" Mom said urgently, pointing me towards the front door.

I sprinted ahead of her, scared, and fumbled for the door knob. I was convinced someone would come flying down the stairs and attack me at any second and that my childhood nightmare of being broken in on was about to come true.

Nobody came.

We both made it outside in a matter of seconds and stood together on the dark sidewalk in the wind. She left the front door open.

"What are we going to do?" I cried. I looked at our car and just wanted to jump into it and drive away, never to return. Couldn't we just leave?

"We'll go across the street and wait for Jackie," she said. "He'll be here in a minute."

"Can't we just go to Betty's?" I asked. "Can't we just go stay with her tonight?"

"Shhh," she replied. "Everything will be fine. It's probably just a mouse."

But everything was not fine. I was terrified. There was something in our house and it knew we were in there, too. It had listened to us and felt our presence as strongly as we'd felt it's. Of that I was sure.

For the next fifteen minutes we huddled there together in the cold, neither one of us had brought our coats, and waited for Jackie to come home. Our eyes never left the house. If someone had been upstairs we would have seen them come down the staircase or at least cross over the stained glass window. We didn't see a thing.

As soon as Jackie arrived I flew at him, giving him pieces of the story in spurts. "It was awful," I said. "And I think there's still someone in there!"

We didn't have a weapon of any kind, so as the three of us (Jackie in the lead) went back into the house he grabbed a broom standing against the wall. He started with the upstairs, with us right on his tail. As he turned on the lights and opened closet doors and peeked under beds, I cowered next to Mom, certain I'd have to make another mad dash for the front door again when someone jumped out and attacked him.

He went through the entire house and nothing was out of order. All the windows were closed and locked. The other exits to the house were blocked by boxes. Nobody was there.

I went on strike after that night, refusing to sleep even with Mom anymore. I didn't feel safe. What if it came back in the middle of the night? Mom couldn't fight off an intruder, much less a ghostly one.

For the first two nights after that I stayed awake all night, keeping some sort of childish vigil as I listened to every noise around me. I wanted to be awake and ready should something come for us. I sat up in the bed, sometimes reading, and waited expectantly for what I knew would happen. Each sound was another pinprick on my skin, causing me to shudder and draw inside even more.

I couldn't go on like that without any sleep, but even Mom was spooked now. She was angry with me at first for not wanting to sleep but after a couple of nights she wasn't able to close her eyes, either. "Let's just not sleep in this room anymore," she suggested. "Maybe another room would be better."

We moved from her bedroom to the living room after a few nights. The fold out bed wasn't comfortable but it was a little warmer in there and at least we were closer to Jackie. I suppose that him being a man made me feel safer somehow. I was able to get a little more rest, even though I continued to wake up every few hours and had difficulty going back to sleep.

Nightly Sounds

*M*oving into the living room worked at first. The only room that separated us from Jackie's room was the kitchen. I also liked the fact that we were able to close all the doors leading into the living room. It made me feel shut-in and secure.

It didn't take long, though, for things to change.

I'm not sure at what point I began waking up and hearing a change in the noises in the house, but it was definitely after we stopped sleeping in Mom's bedroom. The "old" noises were spooky: creaks, clatters, and moans. Technically, though, all of those could be explained by the fact that the house was an old one and bound to make some kinds of noises. I explained them to myself a lot–several times a day, in fact.

The "new" noises were a lot different.

One night, as I was lying in bed on the verge of sleep, a soft scuttle darted across the floor. I opened one eye, half expecting to see a mouse in the floor. There was nothing there.

Upon closing my eyes, the noise started again. This time it came all the way up to the bed, Mom's side, and stopped before slowly backing away and fading into the kitchen. I tried not to think of the fact that it sounded exactly the way I did when I was running across the floor in socks.

A few nights later, a banging noise in the parlor woke me up from a deep sleep. A little disoriented, I rolled over and tried to open my eyes as I forced myself to wake up. I poked my mother in the back, trying to wake her up as well, but we were both so exhausted it was hard to get moving. Then, in the softest of voices, I heard a woman softly whisper, "Just let them sleep."

Well, that made me sit up straight. I turned on the lamp closest to me and looked around the room. Nobody was there. Mom was also up on her feet, looking around. "You heard that, right?" I asked her anxiously.

She nodded.

We slept with the lights on for the rest of the night.

Over the course of the next few weeks we heard sounds that could sometimes be explained and sometimes not. It would often sound as though more than one person was walking through the rooms in our house, only stopping to look in on us while we pretended to sleep. Sometimes, we heard whispers. We couldn't always make out what they were saying, but it was evident whoever "they" were knew we were there and were watching us.

On our way to school in the mornings, we'd talk about what we'd heard the night before.

One morning I cried all the way to school. "I'm scared. I don't want to sleep there anymore. Can I go stay with Betty?"

"Maybe we can sleep in Jackie's room," Mom suggested. "We can move a mattress in there."

And so we did. While Mom began her hunt for the next house, the three of us shared a bedroom as Mom and I slept on a mattress in the floor every night. Jackie must have questioned why we wanted to move into his room, but I don't remember the conversation at the time. Maybe Mom told him it was for the heat. Or maybe she told him the truth.

Because he was scared, too.

Moving Again

My worst fear at the time was that we'd continue to stay on in the house, despite the fact that I was afraid to use the bathroom, afraid to play in my bedroom, and now afraid to sleep. I was afraid things weren't bad enough yet and that we'd stay there until something horrible happened and there wasn't a way out at all.

I couldn't even listen to the "Drinking Champagne" song anymore without breaking out into a cold sweat, just remembering the rocking chair and the way it moved back and forth without another person around it. Sometimes, when it came on, I was afraid other furniture would start moving as well, as though it might have been the song that caused it.

Luckily, the tides changed and a new house was soon on the horizon. Before Thanksgiving rolled around Mom found us a house in the next county over, not far from our school. It didn't even take us long to pack. Since we'd barely unpacked in the first place, there wasn't a lot left to do. I threw most of my stuffed animals in garbage bags. My cousin April came over and helped me. We did it in the middle of the day, with the radio blasting. I think it was the fastest either one of us had ever moved. We weren't going to stay upstairs any longer than we needed to.

I was particularly happy about moving because it meant our cat might start staying inside with us again. It refused to come into our house and would hiss when I tried to bring him. After the first few weeks, I'd given up and let him live outside. I missed him, though. As soon as we got him to the new place he darted in and found a sunny corner in my new bedroom to wrap himself up in.

All moves are long, painful, and tedious but this one was as painless as possible. Jackie had made friends with the manager and co-manager of the local Subway restaurant, just because he went there a lot, and they helped him move the heaviest furniture. We put a lot of things in storage, including most of my toys and summer clothes. It was 1990 and we figured we'd get them out in a few months when the weather warmed up. We didn't get them out until almost twenty years later. I think it was difficult for us to face some of those belongings once they were out of sight. Even as an adult they were a painful reminder of those four months.

I wasn't sorry to say goodbye to the house. Once all the rooms were cleared, however, I did take another walk through it. I was angry now, angry that we hadn't been able to live there and be happy. I wanted to love it. I had been prepared to love it. And now, it looked so innocent when it was bare and devoid of our belongings. Maybe the paint was cracking in a few places and the wallpaper was peeling, but it was an old house with character. I *wanted* to be happy there. I kept repeating that as I walked through the rooms, touching the walls and opening doors.

"Why did you do it?" I asked it as I stood in the middle of the parlor floor. "What did you want from us?"

In answer, my bedroom door upstairs banged shut in finality. I took that as my sign to leave.

Several months later, after we were settled into the new place in Clay City, we went back to visit Betty. Unfortunately, moving away meant we didn't get the chance to visit her as much as we had and we missed her. We were anxious to catch up with her on this visit.

"So," she asked with a big smile once we'd hugged and all sat down. "Are you happier at the new house?"

"Yeah," I said. "A lot. It's peaceful."

"I like it," Mom agreed. "It's different."

"There aren't any ghosts at this one," I said.

Betty laughed. "So no old women on the stairs?" She directed this at Mom.

I looked up in confusion. "What do you mean?"

Both Mom and Betty had sheepish looks on their faces. "Oh, I'm sorry. I thought you would have told her now that you're out of the house," Betty apologized.

"Mom, what happened?"

Mom then went into her own story, one I hadn't been told yet. Apparently, during the first few weeks after we moved in, she was upstairs in the guest room putting away clothes while I was outside riding my bicycle. After a little while, she got the strangest feeling someone was watching her. When she walked over to the landing and looked down through the rails on the staircase, she was surprised to see an old, gray headed woman.

Mom's first thought was that a neighbor had wandered in. She heard we had an elderly neighbor next door who wasn't well. "Are you okay?" Mom asked. "May I help you?"

And with that, the woman disappeared.

Mom had sat down on her bed for almost fifteen minutes, trying to get her bearings and wrap her head around what had just happened. On our next visit to Betty, she'd told her about the experience. She didn't want to tell me because she didn't want me to be scared.

Of course, I had told Betty about the rocking chair, footsteps, and other things I was hearing in the house but hadn't talked about everything with Mom.

If we'd shared tales, we might have moved just a little bit sooner.

The House Today

Fifteen years after moving out, we went back to the house to see how it looked, if it was even still standing. It was. It's currently empty, in fact, and was up for sale recently.

When we first went back and saw it, however, we were amazed at what we encountered. It was in total disrepair. We knew someone moved in when we moved out but they only stayed a short while. After that, it must have been empty for a long time.

The front door was off its frame and the windows were bashed in. My friends Jim and Ashley were with us and while they hadn't heard any of our stories about the house, they were believers in the paranormal (and loved a good old house).

It was difficult to move about the rooms. The floors had rotted through in some places and the ceiling was caving in in others. The claw foot tub where I'd taken many baths was pulled away from the wall and cracked. There was a sink on its side in Mom's old room. The kitchen was in shambles. With so much debris it was hard to even tell what the room had once been. Only the staircase remained untouched. We couldn't go down to the cellar at all, thanks to the weeds that were almost over our heads.

Although it wasn't always a happy place to live, I hated seeing it in that condition. Surely it must have been loved once. But, for whatever reason, nobody wanted to keep it up.

Once we were safely back in the car I asked the others if they'd felt anything in the house. "Oh yeah," Jim answered. "Especially in Becky's room. There's something dark in there and it wasn't happy to see us."

Pulling away, I tried to see it as I had the first time we'd pulled up in the driveway, but it was difficult. It really did look like the scary, haunted house on the block now.

Today, the house has been renovated. It doesn't even look like the same place. Although I haven't been inside, I've seen pictures of it. Someone put in a back deck with a hot tub. New cedar siding covers the front. It appears as though the house has been gutted and new rooms made from the old ones.

Sometimes, I play around with the idea of making an appointment and touring it. But then I'm afraid of taking the chance. What if whatever was there follows me back?

Betty's son Brian passed away a few years after we moved out of the house. He died in the hospital and at his time of death the hospital immediately suffered a power failure. Apparently, nurses on the different floors knew right away Brian had died because of the power situation. They had expected something like that to occur with his passing.

This wouldn't be the last time I saw something or felt something from another realm. But it would be the last time I took those sightings casually. In the past, hearing a noise or seeing something out of the corner of my eye was a good thing; it meant Nana might be nearby. But after living in the Mount Sterling house, I became cautious. I don't know that whatever was there wanted to hurt us, but it felt sinister. I did not feel welcomed in the house. I think it wanted us out. I also think there was more than one spirit in the house. At times I felt a friendliness, a playfulness. Other times, I felt sheer terror and the distinct feeling that whatever was there wanted us gone.

Some people have asked us why we didn't move sooner, why we stayed even as long as we did. The fact is, although a lot of the events happened one right after the other, there were lulls in which nothing happened at all. Much like the body forgets pain, I believe the body also forgets terror. In the clear light of day, when we were away from the house and at school or at Betty's or even just out for a drive it was easy to think about our home with a fondness and without any terror at all. *Things aren't so bad*, I'd tell myself. *It's not as scary as I'm making it out to be.* Several days might go by without anything happening at all and I know I'd be lulled into a false sense of security. I'm not sure how my mother felt, but I imagine it was similar for her. Then, something else would happen and it would be like a slap in the face—a stern reminder that there was something going on within our walls that we just couldn't explain.

Many people have asked me what I thought happened in the house to make it "haunted." The fact is, I don't know. These days, we're accustomed to having closure when it comes to hauntings. On TV shows and in movies there's almost always a "reason" for a place to house ghosts or spirits: someone died there, the house was built atop an ancient Indian burial ground, it was once the site of a Satanic cult's rituals…Unfortunately, in real life, there isn't always a resolution or good explanation for what went on. This leaves us feeling dissatisfied, exhausted, and more than a little frustrated.

I've been asked what the "story" is behind the house, what I think happened there. The truth is, I don't know. I contacted the historical society there in the county but they couldn't point me in any particular direction. No major events occurred in it, at least not any that were documented through the newspaper or other publications that are on file. The town itself is an old one and dates to before the Civil War. The house and grounds, located downtown, have seen many decades and more than a couple of centuries pass by. There's a possibility that it's not the house that's haunted at all, but the grounds around it. I did seek out a few of the neighbors, but they're all new and nobody knows the history of the place. If I could turn back time I'd love to talk to the young man whose grandmother lived in it. I'd like to go back and ask him a ton of questions. But I can't. And I don't even know his name. His grandmother didn't own the house; she was merely a renter.

As a child, I had no interest in the history of the place or the "whys." I only knew that I was scared and wanted out of there. It's important to keep in mind that two decades have passed since we lived in it. It's only been recently that I've become re-interested in the house as a place and not just as a memory from my childhood. My intent with writing these memories down was to try and remember everything that occurred, to have a documentation of sorts, before my memory becomes cloudier and it's more difficult to recall the events that took place there.

Someone told us the house had been used on the Underground Railroad. Historians would say that part of Kentucky wasn't on the route. Others say it was. I have no history on the house but while I think believe it to be at least 100 years old, I'm not sure it predates the Civil War. In the end, I have no explanation for what we saw, felt, or heard there. But the house still stands. And it's still waiting for someone.

Stairwell

My bedroom

Family room

Bathroom

Mom's bedroom

Front of the house

Family room

Uncle Junior

About the author:

Rebecca Patrick-Howard is the author of several books including the first book in her paranormal mystery trilogy *Windwood Farm*. She lives in eastern Kentucky with her husband and two children.

Visit her website at www.rebeccaphoward.net and sign up for her newsletter to receive free books, special offers, and news.

Other books by the author:

Haunted Estill County
More Tales from Haunted Estill County
Finding Henry: A Journey into Eastern Europe
Coping with Grief: The Anti-Guide to Infant Loss
Windwood Farm (Book 1 in Taryn's Camera)
Three Minus One anthology (companion piece to the Lifetime movie *Return to Zero.)*

Windwood Farm excerpt

Book 1 in Taryn's Camera

After several hours of what she thought was pretty good work on her part, she stepped back and admired her own work, gave herself a pat on the back, and took a break. "Well done, old girl," she said aloud and then *literally* gave herself a pat on the back because, after all, she believed if you didn't do it, then nobody else would.

The sun had come out by then and the ground was starting to dry, but it was still very muddy so she headed to the car and sat on the hood while she ate her lunch—leftover Subway from the night before.

Reagan had taken the boards off the windows like she had asked, and now that the sun had risen in the sky it caught the upstairs window and the glare made it appear to wink at her. In fact, it seemed to look right at her. Shielding her eyes, she turned away. "Damn it," she muttered, as she looked at the ground and took another bite. The glare was so bright, however; she couldn't ignore it.

She had grown used to the uneasy feeling she'd developed on the first day and thought she might be making friends with the house. It didn't feel as unwelcoming to her as it did in the beginning and she was almost certain it had even preened a little today while she was painting it, as though it knew it was posing for something that would make it immortal.

Taryn was not a religious person, and wasn't even sure she believed in God, or one powerful entity at all, but she did believe in energy and nature and if there was something bigger than herself in the universe, she always felt it outside when she was alone. She never found it inside the walls of a church or listening to someone preach. Sometimes, while she was painting, she'd get so lost in thought and deep into her picture that she even thought she might becoming a part of it, or with the world around her. It was the closest thing she'd ever had to a religious experience and the feeling of euphoria it gave her was similar to the one she'd gotten off some pain pills when she'd had her wisdom teeth removed.

All of a sudden, a loud crash from inside the house sang out and caused her to jump off the hood and drop her sandwich to the ground. "So much for the five-second rule," she cursed as she watched it immediately get covered with mud and ants. She was hungry, but not *that* hungry.

Still, she was curious about the noise. She didn't think anyone was in the house and it had been a couple of days since she'd been inside. "Eh, why not?" she mumbled, and made her way to the front door. "What's it going to do?"

Always taken a little aback by the amount of darkness that existed even with the windows uncovered, it took her a moment to adjust her eyes when she stepped inside. The living room was cleared of any items and was stark and empty. Taryn thought this made it feel less intimidating than before, as though the boxes had made it feel more lived in, as though someone was coming back. Even the curtains were gone. The peeling wallpaper was still on the walls, though, and it gently flapped as she walked by, stirred by her movements, the only testament to the fact she was actually there.

The hardwood floors were still rock-solid, despite Reagan's concerns, and didn't make a sound as she moved through the rooms. Not a squeak was made. She was surprised by the lack of dust and smiled at the fact that Mrs. Jones had dusted them; that effort was made to sweep the house before it was demolished. It must be a southern thing to clean something before killing it; to fix something before destroying it. She marveled at the beautiful fireplace mantle, so detailed and ornate and yet at the staircase banister, so simple and plain. There seemed to be no rhyme or reason as to why money was spent on some fixtures and not on others. Clearly, the original owners had possessed money, yet had been selective about how it was spent.

The dining room and kitchen were also bare of belongings, as were the downstairs closets. There obviously wasn't anything on the downstairs level that could have made such a loud noise that she heard it from the outside. At any rate, it was as quiet as a church now, or a library. It was hard to imagine this place ever filled with the sounds of a family: laughter, singing, dancing, chattering...Yet the house must have possessed such things and been host to such activities at one time, right? Someone lived in the house and loved it once. Yet there were no echoes of this former life in it now. She could barely even hear own breathing.

Without the boards on the windows and door, it was easier to see. She thought (hoped) the extra light might make the house feel more gracious, yet the welcoming feeling she'd experienced outside disappeared as soon as she stepped through the front door.

Once she circled through the downstairs, she made her way to the first set of stairs in the living room and put her foot on the first step. All at once, a roar so loud, she felt as though her ear drums would pop from the deafening sound filled the room to a raucous level. Staggering, she fell backward and scraped her lower back against the wooden stairs behind her. As she clutched at her chest, she pushed against an invisible force that seemed to thrust against her. The rumble continued all around her, filling the air at an incredible volume, the sound neither man nor animal.

An astonishing wind swept through the room and up the staircase, whipping her hair around her and sending hot air down her throat, making her unable to talk or scream. Gasping for breath, she struggled to talk or breathe and began choking, gagging, wheezing. The front door, which she'd left open, closed with a bang. In horror, she watched small cracks appear in the living room windows and then watched as the glass shattered and flew out into the yard in hundreds of pieces. Using her hands and sheer strength, Taryn managed to grab onto the banister and pull her way up, inch by inch. Finally, by wrapping her legs around the banister, straddling it, and turning her back to the door and wind, she caught her breath. Using what breath she had left, she screamed with everything she had, "WHAT DO YOU WANT!?"

As quickly as it started, everything stopped.

Taryn was left on the banister, like a little kid who had simply been caught sliding down from the top of the stairs. There was utter stillness again with no sign that anything had happened, other than the fact that the windows were broken and the door was closed.

Shaken, she unwound herself from the banister and ran out the front door, not bothering to close it behind her. She'd let the ghost deal with that.

Available from Amazon

Amazon.com: http://www.amazon.com/Windwood-Farm-Taryns-Camera-Book-ebook/dp/B00JRKEFAU/ref=sr_1_1?ie=UTF8&qid=1403281887&sr=8-1&keywords=windwood+farm

Amazon.co.uk: http://www.amazon.co.uk/Windwood-Farm-1-Taryns-Camera/dp/1497550351/ref=sr_1_1?ie=UTF8&qid=1403281967&sr=8-1&keywords=windwood+farm

Printed in Great Britain
by Amazon.co.uk, Ltd.,
Marston Gate.